Good Thoughts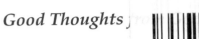

PRAY TO LOVE
LOVE TO PRAY

Prayers, Reflections, and
Life Stories of 14 Great Pray-ers

◆

Biographical Sketches & Prayer Selections
by Carol Graser

Foreword by Father Ed Eschweiler

Hi-Time✳Pflaum
Dayton, OH 45449

In the same way, the Spirit too comes to the aid of our weakness; for we do not know how to pray as we ought, but the Spirit itself intercedes.... And the one who searches hearts knows what is the intention of the Spirit, because it intercedes for the holy ones according to God's will.

Romans 8: 26-27

Art and design by William J. Schueller
Production co-ordinated by Michael F. Vogl
Copyright 1996 by Carol A. Graser

Fourth Printing: September, 2000

Published by Hi-Time✳Pflaum
330 Progress Road
Dayton, OH 45449
800-553-4383

ISBN 0-937997-33-1

CONTENTS

Dedication

Dedicated to our parents and all the other good people who taught us to pray and to take time out now and then to think good thoughts in the Lord's presence.

"Lord, teach us to pray." The apostles are speaking but it could very well be any one of us. Who has not spoken, or at least thought, I wish I could pray better?

Pray To Love, Love To Pray is a delightful little book that can help every one of us to pray better, and it does this in three ways: with life stories, reflections, and prayers.

IN THE LIFE STORIES, Carol Graser brings us brief, inspiring, and credible sketches of fourteen good people. Allowing one page for each, she briefs us on the lives of fourteen good people, most of them canonized saints. Many of these persons are familiar, some may be new to us and some, like St. Francis of Assisi, are enduringly popular. With a marvelous economy of words she enables us to see each of these as people like us who dedicated their lives to doing "something beautiful for God."

Francis of Assisi challenges our values by giving away riches and the life-style of the rich so that he could identify with those he served. We see Elizabeth Ann Seton, first a well-to-do Protestant wife and mother, then a struggling Catholic widow, and finally the one who establishes an American branch of the Sisters of Charity. We learn that Tom Dooley was a typical teenager before entering the navy and later becoming a medical doctor who dedicated his skills and his life to the care of the poor in southeast Asia.

IN THE REFLECTIONS, the author shares with us some good thoughts of these good people. This presents a problem in a foreword—I want to quote so many of them that it would duplicate the book! Allow me, instead, to list a *sample* of themes in these reflections. They touch on the deepest needs and expectations of our lives.

JOY—St. Francis de Sales tells us "A sad saint is a sad sort of saint!" and Mother Teresa gives us assurance that "A person filled with joy preaches without preaching."

TRUST—John Henry Newman writes that God may "hide my future from me—still he knows what he is about."

HOPE—With the simplicity which was so characteristic of her, St. Therese tells us: "As we hope in God, so shall we receive."

SIMPLICITY—Pope John Paul II has said that we need to change our consumerist life-style. St. Elizabeth Ann Seton said it earlier: "Live simply so that others may simply live."

LOVE—Religion is always about relationships, and the greatest of relationships is love. Important as it is for us to love, it is even more important that we understand that God has loved us first. St. Anthony of Padua writes: "One and the same love embraces both God and neighbor, and this love is the Holy Spirit—for God is love." Mother Teresa tells us: "Faith to be true has to be a giving love."

IN THE PRAYERS—Prayer, like our love for God and neighbor, is a response to the love of God in us. All prayer is uniquely personal. It is an expression of who we are, of the kind of God we believe in, and of our relationship to God. Our prayer is sometimes in words, at other times in silence, in listening, in the daily actions of our lives.

Sometimes we pray easily, sometimes thoughts and words do not come. It is at times like these that the prayers selected here can stimulate us. There is also a danger that our prayers may become too comfortable. Here again the prayers in this booklet can help by "stretching" us. Again I offer a brief sampling.

Praying the prayer of St. Augustine with sincerity is a challenge: "Our hearts are made for you, O God, and they will not rest until they rest in you."

Catherine of Siena helps us to realize that we don't even have to know what to ask for as she thanks God "...for having given those things that I never realized I needed or sought."

Teresa of Avila, a mystic, shows us in her prayer that she is also very much in touch with this life: "From all sour faces, O Lord, deliver us!"

And we might want to memorize St. Francis de Sales' invocation: "Lord ... let me love you as much as I can!" and St. Therese's: "Dear Jesus, help me to see only the present and not to worry about the future."

In gathering the material for *Pray To Love, Love To Pray*, the author has performed a great service for us. We live a hurried pace. We are conditioned to instant coffee, microwave cooking, and capsulized news bits on television. This book, in its brevity, can be a grace for the busy people who use it. I hope and pray they will be many.

Father Ed Eschweiler

354-430
Feast Day - August 28
Doctor of the Church

E at, drink, and be merry" was a way of life for Augustine, first in Roman northern Africa where he was born, then in Carthage and Rome where he studied and went to school, and finally in Milan where he gradually began to see the truth about the selfishness of his life. The greatest influences in Augustine's conversion were his mother, St. Monica, who prayed incessantly for him, and St. Ambrose, bishop of Milan, who counseled the young man in his search for truth.

Augustine went on to become a priest, the bishop of Hippo, and one of the greatest thinkers and writers of the Church. In his *Confessions* he gives a deeply personal account of his struggles to renounce a pleasure-seeking and sinful way of living. In *The City of God,* which is considered his masterwork, he fuses classical wisdom and scriptural truths with Church teachings. His influence in the formulation of Christian doctrine has continued through the centuries.

PRAYERS

Pray To Love

Late have I loved you, God,
     O beauty ever ancient, ever new,
Late have I loved you!
     And behold, you were within,
     and I without,
and without I sought you....

You were with me,
     and I was not with you,
those things held me back from you...

You called; you cried;
     and you broke through my deafness.
You flashed; you shone;
     and you chased away my blindness.
You became fragrant;
     and I inhaled and sighed for you.
I tasted,
     and now hunger and thirst for you.
You touched me:
     and I burn for your embrace.

◆

To Mary

O holy Mary,
          who can praise and thank you enough for
          having by your consent brought salvation
          to the world?

◆

Restless

Our hearts were made for you, O God,
and they will not rest
until they rest in you.

◆

Be with Us

Watch, dear Lord, with those
who wake or watch or weep tonight.
Give your angels charge
over those who sleep.

O, Lord Christ,
tend your sick ones,
rest your weary ones,
bless your dying ones,
soothe your suffering ones,
pity your afflicted ones,
shield your joyous ones.
And all, for your love's sake.

◆

God of Life

God of life, there are days
when the burdens we carry
chafe our shoulders and wear us down,
when the road seems dreary and endless,
the skies grey and threatening;
when our lives have no meaning in them
and our hearts are lonely,
and our souls have lost their courage.

At these times, we beseech you, Lord,
flood our path with light,
turn our eyes to where
the heavens are full of promise!

◆

REFLECTIONS

In God's Hands
Leave the past to the mercy of God,
    the future to the providence of God,
        and the present to the love of God.

◆

Keep on Keeping on!
Now let us sing, alleluia,
    not in the enjoyment of heavenly rest,
    but to sweeten our labor.

Sing as travelers sing along the road—
    but keep on walking.

Lessen your work by singing—
    do not give in to idleness;
    sing, but keep on walking.

And what do I mean by walking?
    I mean *press on from good to better...*
    go forward in virtue,
    in true faith, in right conduct.

So sing up—and keep on walking!

◆

Joyfulness
The Christian should be an
alleluia
from head to foot!

1182-1226
Feast Day - October 4
Patron of Ecology

During his early years, Francis Bernadone, son of a well-to-do silk merchant, led a band of young reveller friends in extravagant and riotous living. Because rivalries and wars were common among Italy's provinces and cities, on several occasions he joined armed forces representing his home town of Assisi. It was during these times of war that Francis changed his ways. He became more and more aware of the needs of the poor and, after giving away all his possessions (and some of his father's as well), he "married Lady Poverty" and urged the growing numbers of his followers to do the same.

The Order of Francis, or Friars Minor, was thus begun, and from then on, Francis devoted his life to praying, caring for the sick and the poor, and preaching and teaching. Because he believed himself unworthy to be a priest, he was never ordained. Yet, Francis truly was a man of God, his entire life a canticle of joy in the Lord. Many of the prayers and songs he wrote give evidence of how very much he delighted in the Creator's works as revealed in nature. On April 6, 1980, Pope John Paul II named St. Francis patron saint of ecology.

PRAYERS

Peace Prayer

Lord, make me an instrument of your peace.
 Where there is hatred, let me sow love;
 Where there is injury, pardon;
 Where there is doubt, faith;
 Where there is despair, hope;
 Where there is darkness, light;
 Where there is sadness, joy.

O Divine Master, grant that I may not so much seek
 To be consoled, as to console;
 To be understood, as to understand;
 To be loved; as to love;

For it is in giving that we receive;
 It is in pardoning that we are pardoned;
 And it is in dying that we are born to eternal life.

◆

Prayer Before a Crucifix

Most high, glorious God,
enlighten the darkness of my heart,
and give me, Lord,
 a correct faith,
 a certain hope,
 a perfect love, sense and knowledge,
so that I may carry out
your holy and true command.

◆

Canticle of the Sun

O most high, almighty, good Lord God,
    to you belong praise, glory, honor, and all blessing!
    by you alone were all things made.
Praised be my Lord God with all creatures;
    and especially our brother the sun,
    which brings us the day and the light;
    fair is he and shining with great splendor:
    O Lord, he signifies you to us!
Praised be my Lord for our sister the moon,
    and for the stars
    which God has set clear and lovely in heaven.
Praised be my Lord for our brother the wind,
    and for air and cloud, calms, and all weather,
    by which you uphold in life all creatures.
Praised be my Lord for our sister water,
    which is very helpful to us,
    and humble, and precious, and clean.
Praised be my Lord for brother fire,
    through which you give us light in the darkness;
    and he is bright and pleasing, and very mighty,
        and strong.
Praised be my Lord for our mother the Earth,
    which sustains and keeps us,
    and yields diverse fruits, and flowers of
        many colors ....
Praised be all who are found walking by your most
        holy will,
    for death shall have no power to do them harm.
Praise you, and bless you the Lord and give thanks
        to God,
    and serve God with great humility!

◆

REFLECTIONS

Staying Close to God

Nothing must keep us back,
        nothing separate us from God,
        nothing come between us and our Lord.
At all times and seasons,
        in every country and place,
        every day and all day—
We must have a true and humble faith,
        and keep God in our hearts,
        where we must love, honor, serve,
        praise, bless, glorify and thank
        our most wondrous and infinite Lord—
                Three and One:
        Father, Son, and Holy Spirit forever!

◆

Words Fail!

Let us know, love, adore, serve, praise, bless,
glorify, exalt, extol, and thank our Creator God—
        unchanging, invisible, unutterable,
        incomprehensible, unplumbable, ineffable,
        blessed, praiseworthy, glorious, sublime,
        merciful, loving, delightful, uplifted,
        completely to be desired for all eternity—
And let us be forever grateful that this unspeakable
        greatness, glory and grandeur of our God
have been made more knowable and reachable to us
        through our friend and savior Jesus Christ!

◆

ANTHONY OF PADUA

1195-1231
Feast Day - June 13
Doctor of the Church

Anthony, whose baptismal name was Ferdinand, was born in Lisbon, Portugal, the son of a knight of the king's court. Despite his courtly surroundings, the young boy studied Scripture and became deeply devoted to Jesus Christ. At the age of 15, he left behind family riches and entered the Augustinian Order in Lisbon. He took the name of Anthony and, for several years, lived a solitary life of prayer and Scripture study. But when he met five young Franciscans who shortly thereafter were martyred in Morocco, he changed his life, joined the Order of Franciscans, and vowed to live a life of action as well as of prayer.

Anthony then became a fiery preacher for the Lord. As his fame spread, he was sent to work among the rich and poor throughout Italy. Inspired with the love of Christ, he embraced a life of poverty for himself and preached a message of conversion, repentance, and charity to the throngs that gathered. This "Patron of the Poor" remains today one of the Church's best-loved and most-prayed-to saints—a true friend to persons with all sorts of needs.

REFLECTIONS

True Love

One and the same love
   embraces both God and neighbor,
And this love is the Holy Spirit—
   for God is love.

◆

Look to Jesus

With his arms outstretched upon the cross,
   Christ covers as with wings
   all who ask for help.
Let us lift up our eyes to him.
Let us gaze upon the author of our redemption—
   Jesus!

◆

Caring

As the sail drives a ship,
so let your compassion and concern
lead you to care for the needs of your neighbor.

◆

Mirror

Nowhere can we more clearly grasp our dignity
     than in the mirror of the cross.
If once more we look into it, we can see our true worth,
     since such an inestimable price was paid for us!

◆

Saints

The holy life of each saint
     is like the sun shining upon a temple—
     for in its rays we see the dust of our defects.
We celebrate the feasts of saints
     so that we may find in their lives
     a model for our own.

◆

God's Handiwork

If things created are so full of loveliness,
     how resplendent with beauty
     must be the one who made them!
The wisdom of the worker is apparent
     in the handiwork.

◆

1347-1380
Feast Day - April 29
Doctor of the Church

Catherine Benincasa had a mind of her own. As the youngest of 25 children born into a middle-class Italian family, she made it clear to her parents, who wanted her to marry and have a family, that she preferred a life of celibacy, prayer, and penance. Though she was a bright, witty and well-liked teenager, she spent most of her time praying, meditating, and preparing herself for a life of serving others. When a terrible plague struck the people of Siena, Catherine left home to nurse and minister to the poor and sick in hospitals. Because of her magnetic personality and utter devotion to the Lord, she soon developed a following of admirers who affectionately called her "Mama."

Over the years, "Mama" became an adviser to popes, bishops, priests, and laity. During a time of crisis in the Church when two men claimed to be pope, she was called upon to help settle the problem. Through it all she remained a friend of the poor and neglected. Her correspondence, prayers, and other writings are studied and read to this day.

Dear Ones

O loving God, I wish to pray especially
for the persons you have given to me in my life,
those I dearly love....
I earnestly pray that they will travel
all the way with you on the sweet and straight road
that leads in the end
to the joys of everlasting life. Amen.

◆

Our Part

To you, eternal God, everything is possible,
and even though you have created us
without our help—
you will not save us if *we* do not help!

◆

To the Father

O tender Father,
you gave me more, much more,
than I ever thought to ask for.
Thank you!

And again, thank you, Father,
for having granted my requests,
and for having given those things
that I never realized I needed or sought!

◆

To the Son

Beloved Jesus Christ, the more I love you,
the more you dwell in my heart—
the greater is my longing for you.
If I look upon you forever, it is never enough.
For love of you, I wander through the world
singing and rejoicing!

◆

To the Holy Spirit

O Holy Spirit, come into my heart.
By your power, draw me to you,
true God!
Give me love and reverence for you,
Guard me from all negative thoughts,
Warm me, inflame me with your love,
great God!
Help me now in all that I do,
Spirit, you are my love
you *are* Love!

◆

The Truth About God

God loves us beyond what words can say
and loved us before we ever were.
God created us so that we might enjoy
life with him forever!

◆

The Book of Life

The crucifix is the book of life,
the great book lying wide open,
in which all can read the love of God
and the horror of sin.

◆

The Way to Heaven

There is no way to heaven except this:
to lose oneself, to seek the glory of God,
the salvation of souls, the peace of nations.

◆

It is heaven all the way to heaven!

Suffering

Suffering will heal me;
suffering will grant me light;
suffering will give me wisdom.

◆

Pray Always

We can never reach holiness
or obtain any virtue
without the help of humble, faithful,
and persevering prayer.

◆

Judge Never

For *no* reason whatsoever should we judge
the actions or motives of others!

◆

God's Love

Everything that happens to us or to others
comes from God
and was born of the great love
which the Creator has for all creatures.

◆

1491 - 1556
Feast Day - July 31
Patron of Spiritual Exercises
and Retreats

orn into a noble Basque family, the young soldier "Inigo" seemed to value courting ladies and winning battles for Spain more than anything else in life. However, after his legs were shattered in battle and he was sent home to recuperate, he began to reconsider priorities. With time on his hands, he read Scripture and the lives of the saints. He prayed and reflected and became determined to change his life. First on his agenda was a pilgrimage to the Holy Land. Inigo the soldier had become Ignatius the pilgrim, the penitent, and eventually, the founder of a new order of priests.

In the years after his conversion, Ignatius, with a small group of followers that included Francis Xavier, established the Society of Jesus, better known today as the Jesuits. *The Spiritual Exercises*, which he developed during a ten-month period of prayer and penance, are considered even today the ultimate "textbook" for use during times of prayer, recollection, and retreat.

PRAYERS

Gifts

Take, Lord, and receive
    my liberty, my memory,
    my understanding, my entire will,
    everything that I have and possess—
    you have given all to me.
To you, Lord, I return it.
Dispose of it according to your will.
Give me your love and your grace—
    these are enough for me.

◆

Soul of Christ

Soul of Christ, sanctify me.
    Body of Christ, save me.
Blood of Christ, inebriate me.
    Water from the side of Christ, wash me.

Passion of Christ, strengthen me
    O good Jesus, hear me.
Within your wounds hide me.

In the hour of my death, call me,
    And bid me come to you.
That with your saints I may praise you
    Forever and ever. Amen.

◆

Communion
Lord Jesus, through the Eucharist
    you are, you live, you act in me
    so that I may
    live, feel, think, and act in you.

◆

With God's Help
Dearest God,
    teach me to be generous,
    teach me to serve you as you deserve—
        to give and not to count the cost,
        to fight and not to heed the wounds,
        to toil and not to seek rest,
        to labor and not ask for reward—
    except to know that I am doing your will.

◆

Honoring Mary
Immaculate Virgin, mother of our Savior,
    I honor in you the splendor
    of salvation worked by your Son!

◆

My Needs
Lord, what do I desire,
    or what can I desire,
    besides you?

◆

REFLECTIONS

Mantra
I love God;
I am loved by God!

◆

Finding God
The more our soul is alone and by itself
the more capable it becomes
of drawing near and attaining
its Creator and Lord.

◆

Looking Within
I could no longer live at all
if I did not feel in my soul something *living*
which does not come from myself,
which could not come from myself,
which comes purely from God!

◆

Powerful Medicine
Laugh and grow strong!

1515 - 1582
Feast Day- October 15
Doctor of the Church

Teresa Sanchez, born near Avila in Castile, Spain, was a woman of action and of prayer. Because she was a joyful, bright, witty, and very outgoing person, her townspeople were somewhat surprised when she entered the local Carmelite convent in Avila. In the years that followed, however, as she brought much-needed reform to existing Carmelite convents, or as she established new ones, not only the people of Avila but also of Spain and the Church in the western world came to recognize her leadership abilities.

Early on, Teresa had come to realize that action must be based on a firm foundation of prayer—as she said: "Without contact with God, no good thing is accomplished." Her writings bear out her convictions about the need for times of quiet prayer and reflection. Her most famous work, *Interior Castle*, and other writings are even today considered classics on the spiritual life. These accomplishments were finally recognized in 1970 when Pope Paul VI declared her a Doctor of the Church.

PRAYERS

God's Comforting Presence

Let nothing trouble you,
Let nothing frighten you,
all is passing—
God alone is unchanging;
patience obtains everything.
If you possess God, you want nothing—
God alone is sufficient!

◆

The Wonders of Creation

My gracious God,
May you be blessed forever,
May all your creatures praise you!

◆

Everything To Lose

O, Lord of my soul,
if only someone could find the words to make
others understand what you give to those who
have faith in you, and what they lose who find that
very faith and still hang back!

◆

Whatever It Takes

Dear God, who foresees all,
    please provide whatever it will take
    for me to serve you according to your will
    and not my own.

◆

Short, to-the-Point Prayer

From all sour faces,
O Lord, deliver us!

◆

REFLECTIONS

When You Worry

Remember that—
    you have only one soul;
    you have only one death to die;
    you have only one life, which is short
    and has to be lived by you alone;
    there is only one glory which is eternal!
If you do this—
    there will be many things
    about which you will care nothing!

◆

Genuine Love

We cannot know whether we love God—
though there may be strong reasons for
thinking so.
But there can be no doubt about whether we love
our neighbor—
in proportion as we advance in charity,
we are increasing our love of God!

◆

Don't Feel Like Praying?

Sometimes when you want to escape from prayer,
don't give it a second thought.
Just thank the Lord for whatever desire to pray
that you do have....
When you don't feel like praying,
just go outdoors where you can see the sky,
and take a walk.
Doing that will not be deserting prayer—
and, in fact, can lead you to a *better* prayer!

◆

Faithful Friend

Put all your trust in our good Jesus,
serve him as best you can—
and you shall lack nothing,
for he will *never* desert you.

◆

Peace

Any unrest and stress can be endured
    if we find peace where we live....
Any good thing that we do has its source,
    not in ourselves but in this spring
    called the soul....
As we gradually get closer to the place
    in our soul where God dwells,
      the Creator becomes our very good neighbor!

◆

Necessary Ingredients

Joy is as necessary to holiness
    as are faith and good works!

◆

We have to serve God in God's way,
    not in ours.

◆

Love does everything!

◆

How friendly we'd all be with one another
    if nobody were interested
    in money, fame, or honor!

◆

The ways of God never fail to amaze me.

◆

FRANCIS DE SALES

1567- 1622
Feast Day - January 24
Doctor of the Church
Patron of Catholic Journalists

F rancis de Sales was the kind of preacher that people don't forget. Born into a well-to-do family from the Chateau de Sales in Savoy, France, he was trained and educated as a lawyer though he had always wanted to become a priest. At his father's urging, Francis studied law at the University of Padua and accepted a prestigious legal position. His yearning for ordination persisted, however, and after a time he finally convinced his father that his priestly vocation was genuine.

Ordained in 1594 during the unsettling times of the Protestant Reformation, the zealous young priest was sent to Chablais on Lake Geneva to minister to lapsed Catholics, and it was there that his fame not only as a preacher but also as a confessor and an inspired writer quickly spread.

Crowds gathered wherever Father Francis went because they recognized that he spoke with love. They liked his often-repeated message that holiness is possible for ordinary people in day-to-day living. By his own example as a priest and later as bishop of Geneva, he showed them that simplicity, patience with self, and cheerfulness are the "stuff of sanctity."

My Gift

Lord, at every instant
of my brief existence here on earth,
let me love you
as much as I can!

◆

Hope

Dear God,
When my problems seem more
than I can bear,
I shall go on in courage,
and hope in you
against all human hope.

◆

Great Expectations

With expectation
I have waited for you, Lord,
and you have heard me!

◆

Never Alone

You are my God;
I rely on you, my help, my trust.
I am not afraid because you are with me—
in fact, you are *within* me,
and I in you!

◆

REFLECTIONS

Service with a Smile

When doing for others,
do so as joyfully as you can—
an act of kindness done joyfully and well
will be doubly helpful!

◆

Trust in God

Do not be afraid
about what may happen tomorrow;
the same loving God
who cares for you today
will take care of you tomorrow
and every day.
God will either shield you
from suffering
or give you unfailing strength to bear it.
Be at peace, then,
and put aside all anxious thoughts
and misgivings.

◆

Friends

A friendship founded in God
never dies or fades,
and will remain strong whether the friends
are together or apart...
Good people cultivate noble friendships.
How beautiful it is to be as dear to one another now
as we shall be one day in eternity!

◆

A Good Disposition

We may be forgiven
if we are not always cheerful,
for this isn't always in our power.
But it is unforgivable if we're not always
kind, yielding and considerate—
for this we can always manage.

◆

Taking Risks

It is not necessarily the timid souls
    committing the least number of faults
    who are the most holy.
More often than not it is those persons having
    the greatest courage,
    the greatest generosity,
    and greatest love—
those who make the boldest efforts
    to move forward,
    even at the risk of tripping,
    or even falling and getting dirtied a little!

◆

Food for Thought

Life is short and yet of untold value,
for in it is hidden the germ of eternity.

◆

One kind word
wins more willing service
than a hundred orders or stern reproofs!

◆

The measure of love
is to love without measure!

◆

Nothing is so strong as gentleness,
Nothing so gentle as real strength.

◆

A sad saint
is a sad sort of a saint!

◆

ELIZABETH ANN SETON

1774 - 1821
Feast Day - January 4

A s the first canonized saint born in the United States, Mother Elizabeth Ann Seton holds a special place in the history of the Catholic Church in America. During her relatively short life, she was a socialite, wife, mother, widow, convert, founder of a religious community, and a pioneer in establishing a Catholic parochial school system.

Born into a well-to-do Protestant family in New York, "Betty" Bayley, at age nineteen, married William Seton, a successful merchant. Together, they raised a family of five children. All was going well until illness struck William. When a physician recommended a sea voyage for the ailing husband, the couple set out for Italy. They stayed with Catholic friends who gave great support to Betty as her husband's condition worsened. After his death in 1803, she stayed in Italy for a time, and with God's grace and the support of these Catholic friends, the young widow began her quest for truth in the Catholic Church.

After Elizabeth's reception into the Church, she struggled to support her family, first as a teacher in New York and later in Baltimore where she opened a school. With the help of Bishop John Carroll and other priests, she established and became the first superior of an American branch of the Daughters of Charity. Mother Seton was beatified by Pope John XXIII in 1963, and canonized by Pope Paul VI in 1975.

PRAYERS

Birthday Wish for a Child

May God bless you, my child forever—
your mother's soul prays to God
to lead you through this world,
so that we may come to the heavenly
kingdom in peace
through the merits of our blessed Savior.

◆

At a Daughter's Baptism

This day my little one is received
into the Ark of our Lord—
She has been blessed!
May she remain in the number
of God's faithful children
that being steadfast in faith,
joyful through hope,
and rooted in charity,
she may cross the waves of this world,
and finally enter
the land of everlasting life!

◆

Death of a Spouse

Well, dear God, I am alone.
Yet how can I be alone
while clinging fast to you
in continual prayer and thanksgiving?

◆

Prayer for Fidelity

My God, my Father—
Permit me to bless you
as long as I live;
Permit me to serve and adore you
as long as I breathe!

◆

REFLECTIONS

Disappointments

In every disappointment, great or small,
let your heart fly directly
to your dear Savior,
throwing yourself in his arms
for refuge against every pain and sorrow.
He will never leave or forsake you.

◆

There can be no disappointment
where the soul's only desire and expectation
is to meet God's will and fulfill it!

◆

Keep It Simple!

Live simply
so that others may simply live!

◆

New Venture

If this new venture succeeds, I bless God;
    if it does not succeed, I bless God—
    because then not succeeding will be right.

◆

Link by Link: the Blessed Chain

One body in Christ—he the head, we the members,
    One faith—by his word and his Church,
One baptism—and participation in his sacraments,
    One hope—him in heaven and eternity,
One spirit diffused through the Holy Spirit in us all—
    One God—our dear Lord,
One Father—we his children—
    God above all, through all, and in all.
Oh, my soul, be fastened
    Link by link—strong as death!

◆

A ny potential convert hesitant about taking the final steps toward Catholicism might do well to study the life and writings of John Henry Cardinal Newman. Born into a middle-class London family, Newman and his brothers and sisters were encouraged by their Anglican father and Calvinist mother to read the Bible daily. As a teenage student who enjoyed reading and violin playing more than anything else, John had no particular interest in religion. However, after receiving a full scholarship to Oxford, Trinity College, the young Anglican became intensely interested in Scripture and in moral and religious problems, and increasingly concerned about what he perceived to be the laxity and indifference within his Church.

During the next years, Newman became a tutor and vice-principal of a small college, and as an Anglican preacher, the vicar of the Oxford parish church. Though uncertain about papal authority, he read and studied more and more about the Catholic Church. Finally, with continued research, frequent dialogue with others, and, as he said, "fervent petitions to the Savior," he entered the Catholic Church in 1845.

Newman humbly and faithfully served the Church during the next 45 years, first as a priest ordained in 1846, then as a bishop and cardinal. As rector of the Catholic University at Dublin, he emphasized the importance of spiritual as well as intellectual growth for college students.

To Jesus

Dear Jesus,
    help me to spread your fragrance everywhere.
    Flood my soul with your spirit and life.
    Penetrate and possess my whole being so utterly
        that all my life may be only a radiance of yours.
    Shine through me and be so in me
        that every soul I come in contact with
        may feel your presence in my soul.
    Let them look up and see no longer me,
        but only Jesus!

◆

In the End

Jesus, if I come to you,
    not seeking a sign but determined
    to go on seeking you, honoring you,
    serving you, trusting you,
    whether I see light, feel comfort,
    measure my growth, or not,
    I shall find, even while I am seeking,
    before I call, that you will answer me,
    and I shall in the end
    find myself saved wondrously!

◆

Winding Down

We ask you, dear Lord,
    to support us all the day long
    till the shadows lengthen and evening comes,
        when the busy world is quiet,
        the fever of life is over,
        and our work is done—
    then, in your mercy, give us a safe home,
        a holy rest, and peace at last.

◆

REFLECTIONS

Jesus Came

Jesus came in the dark,
>in the dark night was he born,
>in a cave where cattle were stabled,
>there he was housed;
>in a rude manger,
>there first he laid his head....
But he meant not to remain there,
>resigning himself to obscurity;
>He came into that cave to leave it!

◆

An Unseen World

Though I am in a body of flesh, a member of this world,
>I have but to kneel down reverently in prayer,
and I am at once in the society of saints and angels—
>and I have their sympathy....
The world of spirits, though unseen, is present,
>present, not future, not distant—
it is not above the sky;
>it is not beyond the grave—
>it is here and now;
>the kingdom of God is among us!
Here is a practical truth,
>which should influence our conduct:
"Our conversation is in heaven;
>our life is hid with
>Christ in God."

Our Next Move
Where we go hereafter
depends on what we do after here!

◆

My Mission
God has created me to do some definite service;
he has committed some work to me
which he has not committed to another.
I have my mission—
I may never know it in this life,
but I shall be told it in the next.

I am a link in a chain,
a bond of connection between persons.
He has not created me for nothing.
I shall do good;
I shall do his work.

Therefore, I shall trust him,
whatever and wherever I am.
I cannot be thrown away.
If I am in sickness,
my sickness may serve him;
in perplexity,
my perplexity may serve him;
if I am in sorrow,
my sorrow may serve him.
He does nothing in vain.

He knows what he is about.
He may take away my friends.
He may throw me among strangers.
He may make me feel desolate,
make my spirits sink,
hide my future from me—
still he knows
what he is about.

◆

THERESE OF LISIEUX

1873 - 1897
Feast Day - October 1
Patron of Missions

Therese Martin of Lisieux is a saint for ordinary people. Born into a bourgeois French family, she was the youngest of five daughters raised by very strict parents who were, first and foremost, devout Catholics. Friends and neighbors were not surprised when, one-by-one, each of the daughters entered a nearby cloistered Carmelite convent. There were a few raised eyebrows, however, when at age 15 Therese asked for and received permission to enter the same convent.

As Sister Therese of the Child Jesus, this very young nun went on to show by her day-to-day living that, although God calls each of us to sainthood, we probably will not be called upon to do great dramatic things. Rather, our "sainthood" will come in day-to-day living of the Gospels in our little corner of the world. In her autobiography, *The Story of a Soul*, Therese wrote that "what matters in life is great love, not great deeds." Because she offered many of her prayers and "small deeds" for missionaries, Therese has been declared a patron of missions by the Church she served so well.

The People in My Life

Just as a swirling river rushing down to the sea
    carries along with it
    everything it has met in its course,
    so your love, Jesus, is an ocean
    with no shore to bound it—
    and if I plunge into it,
    I carry with me all the possessions I have.

You know, Lord, what these possessions are—
    the souls you have seen fit to link with mine....
    and when I allow this truth
    to cast its spell over me,
    I don't hurry after you in the first person singular—
    all those I love come running at my heels.

◆

What God Wants

I thank you, God, for all the favors
    you have given me...
Whatever you have given has always pleased me,
    even the gifts which appear to be less good
    than those received by others....
Dear Jesus, help me to see only the present
    and not to worry about the future.

◆

Request

Dear God,
I ask you for myself
and for all those I hold dear,
the strength and grace to follow your will,
to accept for love of you
the joys and sorrows of this life,
so that one day we will all be together
forever in heaven. Amen.

◆

Offering

My beloved God
at every beat of my heart
I want to offer myself to you again and again,
until the shadows fall away
and I can tell you of my love
face to face forever!

REFLECTIONS

As we hope in God,
so shall we receive.

◆

When we yield to discouragement,
it is usually because we give too much thought
to the past and to the future.

◆

Help on the Way

Sometimes when I am very tired,
instead of thinking about my own troubles,
I remember that in some faraway country
missionaries may be worn out
by their work as apostles—
so to lessen their weariness,
I offer mine to God.

◆

Treasures

My treasures are the persons it has pleased God
to send into my life,
those God has given me to love and take care of.

◆

Gifts

Whatever God has given me
has always pleased me—
even the gifts which have seemed less good
than those received by others.

◆

Prayer

Prayer is a cry of gratitude and love
spoken equally in joy and sorrow.

◆

When the kindly, good-natured little man, Cardinal Angelo Giuseppe Roncalli, was elected Supreme Pontiff of the Roman Catholic Church in 1958, many people were surprised. They thought that the 78-year old priest represented little more than a compromise between the Church's moderates and conservatives. He would surely be a transitional pope to be succeeded later by someone better known. Yet when he died after a brief five-year pontificate, he had convened Vatican II, opened the windows of the Church to let in the fresh breeze of ecumenism, and inspired the world with his concern for peace and the dignity of every individual.

Born in Lombardy, Angelo was one of 20 children born to poor but loving and devout parents. At an early age, he strongly desired the priesthood, and at the age of 14 entered the Seminary of Bergamo, where he soon became known not only for his scholarship but also for his cheerfulness, concern for others, and deep devotion to Jesus, Mary, and Joseph.

After Angelo was ordained, he taught as a professor at the seminary. Over the years he served as bishop and apostolic delegate in the Balkans, papal nuncio in France, and patriarch of Venice. Wherever he went, whatever he did, people recognized him as a simple, gentle, and spiritual man of God. No one ever guessed that he was to become Pope John XXIII, one of the best-loved and most influential pontiffs of this or any other time.

To the Holy Spirit

Spirit of love, perfect in us
    the work begun by Jesus:
    Enable us to continue his prayer
    for the whole world;
      hasten in each of us a growth of interior life;
      give vigor to our ministry so that we may reach all
        peoples....
Let everything in us be on a grand scale:
    the search for truth and devotion to it;
    readiness for self-sacrifice, even to the cross and
      death....
O Holy Spirit of love,
    may everything finally be according to the last
    prayer of the Son to our heavenly Father:
    Amen, Amen!
    Alleluia, Alleuia!

◆

To Jesus

Jesus Savior, we thank you for having called us
    to share in God's holy mysteries:
Strengthen us ever more in the faith;
    preserve our piety;
    obtain for us forgiveness of sins....
Keep us ever closely united among ourselves;
    confirm in us your truth;
    reveal to us the truths of which we are still ignorant...
Give us tranquil skies
    and the fruits of the earth in abundance
    and keep the whole world in your loving care.
To you, O Jesus,
    together with the Father and the Holy Spirit,
    be glory, honor and blessing forever! Amen.

◆

To Mary, Our Mother

O Mary, Mary, we beg for holiness of life,
 because this is what matters most
 on earth and in heaven:
Turn your loving gaze
 on those of us who are unhappy;
 may the justice of your Son
 turn to mercy for us all;
 may our trust in you be equal to our hope;
 strengthen in us the good principles of Christian
  life....
O Queen, O Mother, we ask for the kind of love
 which is an inexhaustible source of joy and peace.
 Amen.

◆

With the Lord's Help

Lord, I need only one thing in this world—
 to know myself and to love you....
With your help, I feel ready for everything!
I do not seek, I do not desire the glory of this world;
 I look forward to a greater glory in heaven.

REFLECTIONS

Great Book

The great book
from which I must learn with greater care
and love the lessons of divine wisdom
is the crucifix.
I must make a habit of judging all human concerns,
all knowledge, in light of the principles
of this great book....
When I look at the crucifix
I shall feel all my difficulties dissolve!

◆

The Call of Jesus

Jesus calls you to work with him,
to offer your abilities, your efforts,
your intelligence,
for the spread of his kingdom....
Jesus fed the multitudes with five loaves and two fishes;
he knows how to use your contribution
to the apostolate—small as it may be—
to work *wonders!*

◆

Through Mary

The most direct way to Jesus is through Mary.
So I will be all for Mary
so as to be all for Jesus!

◆

On Positive Thinking

I am optimistic by nature
and prefer to dwell on things that unite
rather than on those that tend to separate.

◆

Families

I would like to place my hand on the heads of infants,
look into the eyes of the young,
and encourage fathers and mothers to pursue
their daily tasks.

◆

When you go back to your homes
hug your children for me—
Tell them that it is an affectionate embrace
from the Pope!

◆

Every parish is my family album!

◆

Light

If God created shadows,
it was in order to emphasize the light.

◆

Every believer in this world of ours
must be a spark of light!

◆

Good Advice

Listen to everything,
forget much,
correct little.

◆

Farewell

Love one another, my dear children!
Seek what unites
rather than what may separate you....
As I take leave, or as I say,
"Till we meet again,"
let me remind you
of what is most important in life:
our blessed Savior Jesus,
his good news,
his holy Church,
and truth and kindness—
I shall remember you all
and pray for you.

◆

D
orothy Day was always something of an upstart. As a young woman passionately searching for truth and meaning in her life, she drifted from a rather unconventional lifestyle in Greenwich Village, to a failed marriage, and on to espousal of such causes as women's rights, pacifism, social and racial justice, and workers' rights. Over the years, with God's grace and the help and support of friends, her search slowly but surely led her to a deep love of Jesus Christ, entrance into the Catholic Church, and a special ministry among the poor in New York and other large American cities.

As a social activist and co-founder of the Catholic Worker Movement, Dorothy firmly believed in the Gospel message that Jesus lives in the poor, and that anything we do for them is done for him. And she came to understand that if Christians are to live Christ's teaching at the Sermon on the Mount, they must stay in touch with the Lord through constant prayer. Always grateful for her gift of faith, Dorothy cherished her membership in the Church till the day she died.

REFLECTIONS

No Room for Despair
No one has a right to sit down
and feel hopeless—
There's too much work to do!

◆

Banquet
We cannot love God
unless we love one another
and to love, we must know each other.
We know God in the breaking of the bread,
and we know each other in the breaking of the
bread,
and we are not alone any more.
Heaven is a banquet and life is a banquet, too,
even with a crust, where there is companionship.

◆

Community
We have lived with the poor
with the workers, the unemployed, the sick.
We have all known the long loneliness,
and have learned that the only solution is love,
and that love comes with community.

◆

Joy
What a driving power joy is!

◆

The Love To Come

It is a joyous thing to think of the love to come,
the love of God which awaits us....
where we will know as we are known....
when all our talents and abilities
will be truly utilized—
when we will be truly loved!

◆

Affecting Others

A pebble cast into a pond causes ripples
that spread in all directions—
Each of our thoughts, words and deeds
is like that.

◆

Belonging to the Church

I have never wanted to challenge the Church,
only to be a part of it, obey it, and in return,
receive its mercy and love,
the mercy and love of Jesus....
If the Church is the cross
on which Christ was crucified,
I want to live and die on that cross!

◆

The Need for Prayer and Retreats

I must have these because I am hungry and thirsty
for the bread of the strong.
I must nourish myself to do the work
I have undertaken.
I must drink at these good springs
so that I will not be an empty cistern
unable to help others.

◆

A hero for our times, Doctor Tom devoted his life to serving the medical needs of the poor and sick people of Southwest Asia, especially Laos, Cambodia, and Vietnam.

Born into a middle-class Irish-Catholic family in St. Louis, Missouri, Dooley was a fairly typical teenager of the times. After high school he entered the University of Notre Dame, but his college days ended in 1944, when he joined the navy as a medical corpsman. After his discharge in 1946, he completed studies at Notre Dame, then entered the School of Medicine at St. Louis University. After receiving his M.D. in 1953, he began medical internship in the U.S. Navy Medical Corps. His contact with the Vietnamese began during that period.

As the Communists in the north began moving south, Dooley volunteered to serve on a ship transporting refugees to Saigon. In 1954, he was transferred to a medical unit in Haiphong where he and a small staff ministered to more than 600,000 refugees. After resigning from the navy in 1956, he organized a mobile medical unit, and later hospitals and clinics, throughout the area. His untimely death of cancer did not end his ministry—the Tom Dooley Heritage, Inc., and other organizations continue his work today.

Seeing God

To see God in all things is sometimes hard....
    especially in a materialistic world,
    but here in the jungle it is easier;
    here we can know God a little better,
    perhaps because of solitude....
God is more intimately present in us than we realize.

We ought to shut up a few minutes and seek God.
    Life can signify much—
    we must listen to the voices inside each of us....
I can say that our work takes on more meaning
    when we remember the words,
"Inasmuch as you have done it unto the least of my
    brethren,
    you have done it to me."

◆

To Find Meaning in Life

Seek a channel to be of service
to the people who "ain't got it so good."
Search for an investment of your humanity!

◆

The Divine Spark

I know now why organized godlessness
    never can kill the divine spark
    which burns within even the humblest human.

◆

Believing and Remembering

I have been taught to believe and do believe
    in God's love, goodness and mercy.
And I do know that these qualities can be
    shared by all of us....
I must remember the things I have seen,
    keep them fresh in memory,
    see them again in my mind's eye,
    live through them again and again in my thoughts.
Most of all, I must make use of them
    in tomorrow's life.

◆

Suffering

When the time for suffering comes,
    then the storm around me does not matter.
Nothing human or earthly can touch me.
A wilder storm of peace gathers in my heart.
    What seems unpossessable, I can possess.
    What seems unfathomable, I can fathom.
    What is unutterable, I can utter—
Because I can pray. I can communicate.
How do people endure anything on earth
    if they cannot have God?

◆

Final Prayer

Death isn't extinguishing the candle—
it's just putting out the light before dawn....
My God, if this is the way you want it to be,
this is the way I want it, too.

◆

1910- 1997

Mother Teresa made it known that she disliked being called a "living saint." Nevertheless, most of her contemporaries who have heard or read about her work among the poor, sick, and lonely people of this world think that she is indeed a "saint for our times."

Born in Skopje, Yugoslavia, Agnes Gonxha Bejaxhiu knew at age 12 that she wanted to be a member of the Irish Sisters of Loreto. As a devoted sodalist eager to read about missionary work in distant lands, she knew at age 14 that she wanted to work among the people of India. Some of her hopes and dreams were realized a few years later when, as newly professed Sister Teresa, she was sent to teach young ladies at the Loreto Convent School in India. But the more familiar she became with the needs of Calcutta's poverty-stricken people, the more she knew that she must leave the Sisters of Loreto and establish a new religious community dedicated specifically to meet those needs.

Mother Teresa's Society of the Missionary Sisters of Charity was thus begun. The community now works among the poorest of the poor throughout the world. At Mother's insistence, inscribed at the entrance of each missionary chapel are Christ's words on the cross: "I thirst!" They serve as a reminder to the sisters of their mission "to console Jesus and to quench his thirst for love."

PRAYERS

Jesus My Patient
Dearest Lord, may I see you today and every day
in the person of your sick,
and, while nursing them, minister unto you....
And, O God, while you are Jesus, my patient,
deign also to be to me a patient Jesus,
bearing with my faults,
looking only to my intention
which is to love and serve you
in the person of your sick.
Lord, increase my faith, bless my efforts and work
now and forevermore. Amen.

◆

REFLECTIONS

Today
Tomorrow has not come,
Yesterday has gone—
We have only today
to love God and one another
as God loves us.

◆

Hunger
The hunger for love, for human touch,
is much greater
than the hunger for a piece of bread.

◆

Joy

A person filled with joy
preaches without preaching!

◆

More Joy

Joy is prayer,
Joy is strength,
Joy is love,
Joy is a net of love
by which you can catch souls!

◆

Holy Communion

In Holy Communion we have Christ
under the appearance of bread and wine.
In our work we find him
under the appearance of flesh and blood.
It is the same Christ!

◆

At the Heart

At the heart of silence is prayer.
At the heart of prayer is faith.
At the heart of faith is life
At the heart of life is service.

◆

Faith and Love

Faith is a gift of God.
Without it there would be no life.
And our work to be fruitful,
to be all for God and beautiful,
has to be built on faith....
Faith to be true has to be a giving love.
Love and faith go together—
they complete each other.

◆

Love To Pray!

Feel often during the day
the need for prayer,
and take trouble to pray.
Prayer enlarges the heart
until it is capable of
containing God's gift of himself.
Ask and seek, and your heart
will grow big enough to receive him
and keep him as your own!